Prayers from a Grateful Heart

A 90-Day Quarterly Devotional and Journal

l. d. wells

Foreword by

Rev. William Holmes Robinson, D. Min.

DEDICATION

This book is dedicated to my Lord and Savior Jesus Christ.
Thank You for divine inspiration to serve You faithfully every day.

Scriptures taken from King James Version of the Bible

For Devon
My *Sonshine*. . .I am eternally grateful for you!

CONTENT

INTRODUCTION

Late December 2012 I was sitting in Sunday morning Worship Service at the Word of Faith Family Cathedral. That morning, the leader of our congregation, Bishop Dale C. Bronner, issued a charge that 2012 would be the "Year of Commitment" and challenged each of us to commit to doing something for God every day of the year and to watch how God would bless even the smallest commitment that we make.

Not long after, I was flipping channels and saw a clip of media mogul Oprah Winfrey speaking about how important the concept of gratitude is to her life. At that moment, I decided that my commitment for 2012 would be to simply be thankful for all of the things that God has already done – in writing.

It did not occur to me at the time that my decision to commit to the Lord in prayer would be the making of this devotional. I am thankful that He gave me the idea to share my journey with the world. I stand as a living witness of the goodness of our God. I believe that if you dedicate yourself to Him in a posture of thankfulness, He will bless your efforts.

I wanted everything about this book to be special. It's done in a daily format instead of date format so that you can begin the journey at any time instead of waiting to line up with a calendar! Even the colors of the book cover (yellow and purple) were chosen for their symbolism and the energy they carry. Yellow = faith, healing, intuition and heightened intellect; while purple = spiritual prowess, clairvoyance, and awakening.

Lastly, I wanted the routine to be easy with one page per day. The reader will start with a scripture followed by a devotion that is purposely written from a global perspective. There is space to jot down personal thoughts and finally, a one line declaration that shifts the focus to a personal one.

Enclosed in the pages that follow is installment one of a four volume series. It is my sincere hope that this guide to living a life of gratitude will bless your spirit – as it is the outpouring of my heart.

His Blessings and Mercy Always,

L. D. Wells

ACKNOWLEDGMENTS

All praise to my Lord and Savior Jesus Christ! I am thankful for the wisdom to be obedient to this calling that was deeply shrouded in my spirit. I truly hope that my labor of love touches everyone that reads this just as deeply as I was affected when going through this process.

A world of thanks to my editor, Joy Burson. Not only did she go through each page of this book with a fine-tooth comb, she has been a constant support throughout my entire life. Since age five, she has been there. I have ALWAYS been able to count on her for wisdom and truth. Everyone deserves a friend like Joy. The bonus to our friendship is that she is also able to edit me. ☺ I hope she knows that I thank the Lord for her every day.

Thanks also to my son, Devon, for his patience as I followed the gumption of the Holy Spirit. He witnessed me laughing, crying, shouting, praising and every other emotion possible. He saw me change and grow through this experience and I know that he is also better for it. He took this journey with me and served as both my student as well as my teacher. I can't wait to see the manifestation of what the Lord is doing in his life!

A debt of gratitude to Pastor William Holmes Robinson. Your unwavering support of my work since the 1990s is something that I have grown quite accustomed to, but will never take for granted. I just know that Deacon Robinson and Mrs. Josephine are both smiling down on us from heaven.

Thanks also to Reverend Arthur C. Carson of Springfield Baptist Church. You became my Pastor when I was just four (4) years old and from that point taught me essentially everything I know about the Holy Trinity and the Bible. You've been a spiritual father, teacher and friend. I'm grateful.

Thanks to those who often spent time in ministry with me. I apologize that we often conducted our sessions at awkward hours of the morning ☺ but am glad that we always encouraged each other to "keep going" just when we were ready to give up. I love you guys and this would not be possible if it had not been for you.

Lastly, to everyone this book touches, may you be blessed in immeasurable ways! May you receive the bountiful goodness that a grateful heart brings!

Namaste

Foreword

Pastor William H. Robinson
The Olivet Church
Fayetteville, GA

My Brothers and Sisters,

Gratefulness is miraculous! Scriptures teach us a great deal about gratitude and the need to cultivate a grateful heart. We, as believers, greet one another with grateful attitudes. We proclaim, "I will bless the Lord at all times. His praise shall continually be in my mouth!" We sing great hymns of praise, "Bless the Lord, Oh my soul, and all that is within me. Bless His holy name!" But the question we must ask ourselves is, "Are we truly grateful? Is gratefulness part of our everyday life? Do we really live the lives we sing about?

I challenge you to remember that the word of God is true. He has done great things -- lest we forget. We are commanded to thank God in ALL things. Why do you think that is? Ultimately, it is because it promotes our happiness and well-being. When we begin to unlock this understanding of God's design for us, and fully commit to it, our lives will instantly shift.

1 Thessalonians 5:16–18 teaches:

16 Rejoice always, 17 pray continually, 18 give thanks in all circumstances; for this is God's will for you in Christ Jesus.

This simply means learning to live life as if everything were a miracle, and being aware on a continuous basis of how much we've been given. An attitude of gratitude shifts the focus from what life lacks to the abundance that is already present. We tend to take for granted the good that is already present in our lives.

You may ask, "What about when bad things happen?" Well, it is at these times that a spirit of gratefulness is essential. In fact, when we are in crisis, is precisely when we have the most to gain by a grateful perspective on life. See, it's easy to feel grateful for good things and when life is running smoothly. But . . . I promise you, when we learn to become grateful in ALL things is when we begin to ascend into the higher sphere of the life that was intended for each of us.

Gratitude will shift the narrative of your life! It's the key to experiencing life at its best. When we are grateful for each of our blessings – great and small -- this is what opens the door to a life of success and prosperity.

As the seasons of your life change, it is paramount that you remain able to have the right perspective and understand the value that each cycle of life brings. Doing so will allow you to harness that power needed to go from a life of dread and complaining to a life of peace and appreciation.

If we wish to produce a more meaningful life, we must begin to recognize our blessings and practice gratitude -- even in the worst of times. Be resolved that nothing has the power to take your peace. Be content in all things, knowing, it is the manifest will of God.

It is my fervent prayer that starting today, every heart that begins this 90-day journey to cultivating a grateful heart, will learn to bring gratitude to your own experiences – instead of waiting for a positive experience in order to feel grateful.

Blessings,

Rev. Dr. William Holmes Robinson
Pastor

Day 1

And God saw everything that He had made, and behold it was very good. And the evening and the morning were the sixth day.

Genesis 1:31 KJV

Thank You Lord,

You are molding us into the people You have called and ordained us to be! We are becoming a people fashioned by Your hands to do great things. We are marvelously made and our best days are yet to come. Amen.

ಐ

_____

_____

_____

_____

_____

_____

_____

~Prayer: Thank You Lord for making me in Your image.

Day 2

Wherefore I beseech you, be ye followers of me.

I Corinthians 4:16 KJV

Thank You Lord,

For preparing us to follow You. Thank You for this opportunity to have Your wisdom and guidance lead every decision we make. You are preparing us to do great things in Your name and we are grateful. Amen.

☙

_____

_____

_____

_____

_____

_____

_____

_____

~**Prayer**: Thank You Lord for leading the way for me.

Day 3

And he said, Take now thy son, thine only son Isaac, whom thou lovest, and get thee into the land of Moriah; and offer him there for a burnt offering upon one of the mountains which I will tell thee of.

Genesis 22:2 KJV

Thank You Lord,

We can offer our lives and the lives of our child (ren) up to Christ. We know that we are precious in Your sight and are certain that You are in control of our destiny. Lord we are Yours, and for that, we are grateful. Amen.

CB

_____

_____

_____

_____

_____

_____

_____

~**Prayer**: Thank You Lord for giving me the ability to sacrifice.

Day 4

Therefore I say unto you, Take no thought for your life, what ye shall eat, or what ye shall drink; nor yet for your body, what ye shall put on. Is not the life more than meat, and the body than raiment?

Matthew 6:25 KJV

Thank You Lord,

We don't have to worry about what tomorrow will bring. We can simply trust that all things are working together for the good of those who love the Lord and are called according to His purpose. We love You Lord. We trust You Lord. May Your will be done in our lives, in the lives of our families and friends, and in the lives of future generations to come. Amen.

☙

_____

_____

_____

_____

_____

_____

_____

~Prayer: Thank You Lord for taking away my worries and concerns.

Day 5

But as for you, ye thought evil against me; but God meant it unto good, to bring to pass, as it is this day, to save much people alive.

Genesis 50:20 KJV

Thank You Lord,

Thank You for removing the negative thoughts I harbor against those who have done wrong toward me; or taken advantage of my kindness; and those who have sought to cause confusion by their lies and by "throwing others under the bus" for their own personal gain; and even those who have been deceitful and unreliable. Thank You for giving me peace that allows me to relinquish any anxiety toward these negative influences. Bless every individual Lord, and give them experiences that lead them to live for You. Amen.

CB

_____

_____

_____

_____

_____

_____

_____

_____

~Prayer: Thank You Lord for my deliverance from negative thoughts.

Day 6

And if it seem evil unto you to serve the Lord, choose you this day whom ye will serve; whether the gods which your fathers served that were on the other side of the flood, or the gods of the Amorites, in whose land ye dwell: but as for me and my house, we will serve the Lord.

Joshua 24:15 KJV

Thank You Lord,

We can serve You! Lord, thank You for removing anything that stands between us and You, in the name of Jesus. Lord, You can touch the hearts of those in our family and beyond, who have heard of You, but have not yet chosen to live by Your precepts. We are graced to see Your awesome power in action and how You work miracles. And, when the time comes, thank You for bringing each of us safely into Your kingdom unto eternal life. Amen.

ଓଃ

_____

_____

_____

_____

_____

_____

_____

_____

~Prayer: Thank You Lord for the gift of salvation in my life.

Day 7

Thou shalt have no other gods before Me.

Exodus 20:3 KJV

Thank You Lord,

For entering into our hearts. We are Yours and You show us Your secret mysteries. You draw near to us and allow us to draw near unto You. You're with us – even now. Thank You for cleansing us and giving us a heart for You. We are willing and You have shown us Your great love and truth. Our hearts are a place for Your sacred worship. We forsake all others and worship only You. Amen.

CB

_____

_____

_____

_____

_____

_____

_____

_____

~Prayer: Thank You Lord for making my heart Your home.

Day 8

And he said, I beseech thee, shew me Thy glory.

Exodus 33:18 KJV

Thank You Lord,

Thank You for showing us Your light. You infuse us with the light only You can give and make us an illumination for others who remain in darkness. Continue to show us the way so others can follow us as we follow Christ. Amen.

.

CB

_____

_____

_____

_____

_____

_____

_____

_____

~Prayer: Thank You Lord for shining Your light through me.

Day 9

But my God shall supply all your need according to his riches in glory by Christ Jesus.

Philippians 4:19 KJV

Thank You Lord,

ℰ You have smoothed our individual paths by Your mighty hand of You have smoothed our individual paths by Your mighty hand of provision. Thank You that there has never been a time when our needs have gone unmet. Thank You that you have taught us to determine the difference between a 'want' and a 'need'. We can honestly say that all we have needed Thy hand has provided. Thank You Lord. Amen.

છ

_____

_____

_____

_____

_____

_____

_____

~Prayer: Thank You Lord for supplying all of my needs.

Day 10

In a pan it shall be made with oil; and when it is baken, thou shalt bring it in: and the baken pieces of the meat offering shalt thou offer for a sweet savour unto the Lord. ²²And the priest of his sons that is anointed in his stead shall offer it: it is a statute forever unto the Lord; it shall be wholly burnt.

Leviticus 6:21-22 KJV

Thank You Lord,

You are in control! We have been grasping at our future when we simply need to give it completely over to You. We have allowed ourselves to become angry in our workplaces because we know that what we see right now is not our destiny! In spite of this, we are thankful for Your hand of provision. We are certain beyond a shadow of a doubt that You have ordained great things for our lives. We trust You Lord and will die daily to this flesh that is weak and yearning to know what is next – or even what is right around the corner. We release all anxiety in the name of Jesus. We release these broken pieces. We wait. We believe. We thank You. Amen.

 CB

~Prayer: Thank You Lord for preparing my destiny.

Day 11

Ye shall do my judgments, and keep mine ordinances, to walk therein: I am the Lord your God.

Leviticus 18:4 KJV

Thank You Lord,

We are able to yield our hearts to You in the areas of finance and love. We realize that we cannot handle either of these on our own. While we may have had some success, we have not yet experienced the "abundance" that can only come from having You take charge. Lord, we trust You are providing all that we need. We will continue to look to You and to simply keep Your ordinances. We will live for You. Amen.

℃ℬ

_____

_____

_____

_____

_____

_____

_____

~**Prayer**: Thank You Lord for giving me an abundant life.

Day 12

And Caleb stilled the people before Moses, and said, Let us go up at once, and possess it; for we are well able to overcome it.

Numbers 13:30 KJV

Thank You Lord,

We believe that You are ordering – shifting and moving – things in this season. We believe You have already granted us the desires of our hearts and that we are simply waiting to see the manifestation here on earth of what we already know. In our quiet moments we can see Your hand moving. We can see things working in our favor . . . and for this, we say, "Thank You Lord!" Amen.

☙

_____

_____

_____

_____

_____

_____

_____

~**Prayer**: Thank You Lord for granting me the desires of my heart.

Day 13

But my servant Caleb, because he had another spirit with him, and hath followed me fully, him will I bring into the land whereinto he went; and his seed shall possess it.

Numbers 14:24 KJV

Thank You Lord,

You are helping us to keep a clear mind! We are learning to be more organized and how to secure, save and allocate funds wisely. Thank You for showing us the connection between these things and our ultimate success. Thank You also for showing us how to maintain the balance between work and rest. Lastly, thank You for clearing our minds and removing any blocks to creativity. Thanks also for giving us the spirit to follow You wholeheartedly as You bless our future generations. Amen.

♋

_____

_____

_____

_____

_____

_____

_____

~Prayer: Thank You Lord for giving me a clear mind and spirit.

Day 14

But if ye will not do so, behold, ye have sinned against the Lord: and be sure your sin will find you out.

Numbers 32:23 KJV

Thank You Lord,

You expose those who commit sins against themselves, against others and against Your word. Thank You also for restoring those who have been harmed by the words and actions of others. Amen.

℘

_____

_____

_____

_____

_____

_____

_____

_____

~**Prayer**: Thank You Lord for healing my soul.

Day 15

Then Peter said unto them, Repent, and be baptized every one of you in the name of Jesus Christ for the remission of sins, and ye shall receive the gift of the Holy Ghost.

Acts 2:38 KJV

Thank You Lord,

You promised that if we would repent and be baptized, we would come to know the fullness of Your salvation. Thank You for second chances – or as many chances needed to get things in order. Thank You that when we are weak, You are strong. Thank You for helping us to live righteously before You and for the gift of the Holy Spirit freely given. Amen.

છ

~**Prayer**: Thank You Lord, for giving me the gift of the Holy Spirit.

Day 16

Keep the Sabbath day to sanctify it, as the Lord thy God hath commanded thee.
Deuteronomy 5:12 KJV

Thank You Lord,

You give us divine rest! Thank You for the ability to drop everything and to dedicate ourselves to You in worship and praise. Thank You for the ability to draw near to You. Thank You for receiving our personal praise and adoration and for the peace that comes in exchange. Amen.

 beginG

_____

_____

_____

_____

_____

_____

_____

_____

~Prayer: Thank You Lord for receiving my praise and adoration.

Day 17

Who fed thee in the wilderness with manna, which thy fathers knew not, that he might humble thee, and that he might prove thee, to do thee good at thy latter end;
Deuteronomy 8:16 KJV

Thank You Lord,

You are a provider. You have made provision for all of our needs to be met. Thank You for the ability to cast our cares upon You knowing that You are opening doors for us and ushering us into our destiny. Thank You that the end will be well. Amen.

ॐ

_____

_____

_____

_____

_____

_____

_____

~Prayer: Thank You Lord for meeting my every need.

Day 18

There are many devices in a man's heart; nevertheless the counsel of the Lord, that shall stand.

Proverbs 19:21 KJV

Thank You Lord,

You give each of us purpose! Thank You for the yearning that You have placed in us to accomplish certain goals. Thank You also for Your divine guidance that uses every experience to bring us closer to our purpose. Amen.

༺༒༻

_____

_____

_____

_____

_____

_____

_____

_____

~**Prayer**: Thank You Lord for giving me purpose!

Day 19

God is not a man, that he should lie; neither the son of man, that he should repent: hath he said, and shall he not do it? or hath he spoken, and shall he not make it good?

Numbers 23:19 KJV

Thank You Lord,

You keep Your promises! Thank You for loving us. Thank You for leading and guiding us along this life's journey. Thank You for going before us in every situation and causing us to have the best end result. Amen.

CB

_____

_____

_____

_____

_____

_____

_____

_____

~Prayer: Thank You Lord for always fulfilling Your promise.

Day 20

. . . And Joshua fell on his face to the earth, and did worship, and said unto him, What saith my lord unto his servant?

Joshua 5:14 KJV

Thank You Lord,

We can come to You and inquire about the plans You have for our lives. Thank You for caring for each and every one of us and for giving purpose to us all. Thank You that You have ordained even the smallest of occurrences to benefit us. Amen.

⚃

_____

_____

_____

_____

_____

_____

_____

~Prayer: Thank You Lord for guiding my daily life.

Day 21

Hebron therefore became the inheritance of Caleb the son of Jephunneh the Kenezite unto this day, because that he wholly followed the Lord God of Israel.
Joshua 14:14 KJV

Thank You Lord,

You are restoring, planting and growing Your people! For this reason we no longer have a spirit of anxiety nor fear. Instead we have adopted a "Caleb" spirit because we wholly trust You and are waiting to see the manifestation of Your plans for us. Amen.

ೞ

_____

_____

_____

_____

_____

_____

_____

~Prayer: Thank You Lord for removing fear and anxiety from my heart so that I may wholly trust You.

Day 22

And the Lord said unto Gideon, By the three hundred men that lapped will I save you, and deliver the Midianites into thine hand: and let all the other people go every man unto his place.

Judges 7:7 KJV

Thank You Lord,

You are giving us the wisdom and understanding needed to prepare for the future. Your guidance will give us the jurisprudence to make Godly decisions as we pursue our dreams. Thank You for showing us who to trust, how to work efficiently, and how to make the best use of our skills as we walk into our divine destiny. Amen.

☙

_____

_____

_____

_____

_____

_____

_____

_____

~**Prayer**: Thank You Lord for guidance and wisdom to make Godly decisions.

Day 23

And Ruth said, Entreat me not to leave thee, or to return from following after thee: for whither thou goest, I will go; and where thou lodgest, I will lodge: thy people shall be my people, and thy God my God.

Ruth: 1:16 KJV

Thank You Lord,

You are teaching us how to live life fully! Just like Ruth, we will live for You, go where You lead, and faithfully serve You. We will never turn back and will admonish others to follow us as we follow Christ! Amen.

CB

_____

_____

_____

_____

_____

_____

_____

~**Prayer**: Thank You Lord for the example of Ruth that shows me how to faithfully follow You – and to lead others to do the same.

Day 24

And she vowed a vow, and said, O Lord of hosts, if thou wilt indeed look on the affliction of thine handmaid, and remember me, and not forget thine handmaid, but wilt give unto thine handmaid a man child, then I will give him unto the Lord all the days of his life, and there shall no razor come upon his head.

1 Samuel 1:11 KJV

Thank You Lord,

You are watching over our children! You keep them full of Your love, grace and wisdom. They are protected by Your shed blood on Calvary and no harm shall come upon them. Amen.

C

_____

_____

_____

_____

_____

_____

_____

~**Prayer**: Thank You Lord for extending Your shield of protection to my child (ren) and for keeping all children from all hurt, harm and danger.

Day 25

Thy servant slew both the lion and the bear: and this uncircumcised Philistine shall be as one of them, seeing he hath defied the armies of the living God.

I Samuel 17:36 KJV

Thank You Lord,

We are building faith through every victory! It is in the small trials that You are helping us to trust You with larger tests of our faith. Thank You that every need is met and for rewarding us as we continue to diligently seek You. When there are those around us that would lie, cheat, steal, bully or otherwise do us harm; You are ever present to deliver us. We stand in confidence knowing that You have already provided victory in every situation. Amen.

03

_____

_____

_____

_____

_____

_____

_____

_____

~Prayer: Thank You Lord for giving me victory over wrongdoers!

Day 26

He brought me forth also into a large place: he delivered me, because he delighted in me.

2 Samuel 22:20 KJV

Thank You Lord,

You have delivered us from the enemy as they sought to threaten our peace, joy and confidence. Thank You for lifting us above chaos, trickery or foolishness. Thank You for new seasons, deliverance and for taking delight in us as we trust You. Amen.

Ↄↄ

_____

_____

_____

_____

_____

_____

_____

~**Prayer**: Thank You Lord for taking delight in me.

Day 27

And the three mighty men brake through the host of the Philistines, and drew water out of the well of Beth–lehem, that was by the gate, and took it, and brought it to David: nevertheless he would not drink thereof, but poured it out unto the Lord.

2 Samuel 23:16 KJV

Thank You Lord,

You are our source! We know that anything that we are provided with comes from You. We know that whatever we are given, we can place in Your hands. We pour out to You our praise, our lives, our finances, our children . . . everything. Thank You that no matter how large or small, You are faithful to accept our offering. Amen.

 C3

_____

_____

_____

_____

_____

_____

_____

_____

~Prayer: Thank You Lord for accepting my humble sacrifice.

Day 28

And Elijah said unto her, Fear not; go and do as thou hast said: but make me thereof a little cake first, and bring it unto me, and after make for thee and for thy son.

I Kings 17:13 KJV

Thank You Lord,

You have won our affection! Thank You for wise instruction. We understand that following after Your righteous teaching will cause us to have the best outcome. Even when we don't understand *why* You have given a particular commandment, we *know* that the end result will cause us to triumph and to live more abundantly. Amen.

୯ଓ

_____

_____

_____

_____

_____

_____

_____

_____

~Prayer: Thank You Lord that I can trust You in every situation.

Day 29

And he said, Go forth, and stand upon the mount before the Lord. And, behold, the Lord passed by, and a great and strong wind rent the mountains, and brake in pieces the rocks before the Lord; but the Lord was not in the wind: and after the wind an earthquake; but the Lord was not in the earthquake:

I Kings 19:11 KJV

Thank You Lord,

You show Yourself strong in our lives. Thank You also that You cause us to listen and to pay attention to the things that happen to us that You are not involved in. Thank You for discernment in all matters. Thank You also for the Bible, a tremendous roadmap -- and for the ability to listen to Your still small voice. Amen.

☙

_____

_____

_____

_____

_____

_____

_____

_____

~Prayer: Thank You Lord for discernment in all matters.

Day 30

And Elisha prayed, and said, Lord, I pray thee, open his eyes, that he may see. And the Lord opened the eyes of the young man; and he saw: and, behold, the mountain was full of horses and chariots of fire round about Elisha.

2 Kings 6:17 KJV

Thank You Lord,

You answer our prayers! Even when the answer is not what we seek, You are an ever present help to us. You aid and rescue us. You hear us as we cry out to You. Thank You for always going before us and making provision. Your protection covers us and we are safe in Your arms. Amen.

☙

_____
_____
_____
_____
_____
_____
_____

~**Prayer**: Thank You Lord for answering my prayers.

Day 31

And it shall be, when thou shalt hear a sound of going in the tops of the mulberry trees, that then thou shalt go out to battle: for God is gone forth before thee to smite the host of the Philistines.

I Chronicles 14:15 KJV

Thank You Lord,

You are a mighty warrior and King! Who shall stand against us if Thou art for us? You are mighty in battle and go forth before us to smite the enemy. We are Your faithful cheerleaders. We lift both our heads and hearts in praise to Jehovah Nissi because You reign in victory. Amen.

CB

_____

_____

_____

_____

_____

_____

_____

~**Prayer**: Thank You Lord for being Jehovah Nissi. You reign in victory.

Day 32

If my people, which are called by my name, shall humble themselves, and pray, and seek my face, and turn from their wicked ways; then will I hear from heaven, and will forgive their sin, and will heal their land.

2 Chronicles 7:14 KJV

Thank You Lord,

You are able to cleanse us from all unrighteousness. When we have been covetous and lustful after the things of the flesh, You purge us. Thank You for removing gossip from our lips and helping us to use our words to uplift others instead. Thank You for helping us to replace selfishness with a servant's attitude. Thank You for healing us as we move forward in You. Amen.

೫

_____

_____

_____

_____

_____

_____

_____

~**Prayer**: Thank You Lord for purging me.

Day 33

And when they began to sing and to praise, the Lord set ambushments against the children of Ammon, Moab, and mount Seir, which were come against Judah; and they were smitten.

2 Chronicles 20:22 KJV

Thank You Lord,

You cause our enemies to stumble! You are a way-maker that intercedes on our behalf. Thank You that when we grow weary because of the enemy's constant attacks, we are reminded that these are simply opportunities to trust You. You will show up strong if we only believe. Amen.

☙

_____

_____

_____

_____

_____

_____

_____

_____

~**Prayer**: Thank You Lord for ambushing my enemies.

Day 34

For the builders, everyone had his sword girded by his side, and so builded. And he that sounded the trumpet was by me.

Nehemiah 4:18 KJV

Thank You Lord,

You have given us power to be bold, courageous and vigilant in our pursuit of worthwhile goals. Thank You for the ability to put on our sword and shield of faith. These spiritual weapons – when coupled with our praise – ensure our victory over evil forces seeking to hinder our forward progression. Thank You that You care about what is important to us. Amen.

ᏣᏣ

_____

_____

_____

_____

_____

_____

_____

_____

~Prayer: Thank You Lord for spiritual weapons that aid in my growth and development.

Day 35

Yea, forty years didst thou sustain them in the wilderness, so that they lacked nothing; their clothes waxed not old, and their feet swelled not.

Nehemiah 9:21 KJV

Thank You Lord,

You continue to sustain us. All of our needs are met. We lack nothing. Your hand continues to deliver. Your word declares, "I know the plans I have for You. Plans to prosper You and not to harm You, plans to give You hope and a future." We are grateful. Amen.

ᘓ

_____

_____

_____

_____

_____

_____

_____

_____

~Prayer: Thank You Lord for sustaining me and for planning my future.

Day 36

Now when the turn of Esther, the daughter of Abihail the uncle of Mordecai, who had taken her for his daughter, was come to go in unto the king, she required nothing but what Hegai the king's chamberlain, the keeper of the women, appointed. And Esther obtained favour in the sight of all them that looked upon her.

Esther 2:15 KJV

Thank You Lord,

You have taken time to beautify our souls. You have consecrated us and pulled us apart to be presentable for what the future has in store for us. Thank You for stripping us of people, places and things that serve us no purpose. Thank You for releasing us from thoughts, motives and behaviors that are not like Yours. Thank You for making us ready. We welcome Your purification. Amen.

CB

_____

_____

_____

_____

_____

_____

_____

~Prayer: Thank You Lord for making me ready.

Day 37

Hast not thou made an hedge about him, and about his house, and about all that he hath on every side? Thou hast blessed the work of his hands, and his substance is increased in the land.

Job 1:10 KJV

Thank You Lord,

You keep us safe and secure. We are aware of Your presence in our lives. Thank You for continual guardianship and for never leaving us. In times when we may feel far away from You or have even distanced ourselves because of sin or shame, Your protection still covers us. Amen.

CB

_____

_____

_____

_____

_____

_____

_____

~Prayer: Thank You Lord for keeping me and everyone I love secure.

Day 38

Behold, happy is the man whom God correcteth: therefore despise not thou the chastening of the Almighty: For he maketh sore, and bindeth up: he woundeth, and his hands make whole.

Job 5:17 KJV

Thank You Lord,

You correct us to help make us whole. You remove all complaints from our hearts and help us to focus the same energy in a positive direction. Have Your way with us dear Lord and thank You for showing how You care through divine correction. Amen.

॰

_____

_____

_____

_____

_____

_____

_____

_____

~Prayer: Thank You Lord for making me whole through correction.

Day 39

Though he slay me, yet will I trust in him. . .

Job 13:15 KJV

Thank You Lord,

There is nothing anyone can say or do to cause us not to trust You!
You have proven again and again that no matter what things look like
around us, whatever You have ordained for us is the best possible
outcome. Though You correct us, it is to refine our character and to
cause us to be the best expression of ourselves. Now cause us to be
mouthpieces of Your glory so that others may come to trust You as
we do. Amen.

☙

_____

_____

_____

_____

_____

_____

_____

~Prayer: Thank You Lord for causing me to draw others to You.

Day 40

Acquaint now thyself with him, and be at peace: thereby good shall come unto thee.

Job 22:21 KJV

Thank You Lord,

You are not the author of confusion! Thank You for the calm and gentle spirit that we have been graced to know. If we are experiencing unrest, it is simply because we are not resting in You. Thank You for gracing us to stay in Your peace. Continue to work a great wonder of grace in our hearts and minds. Amen.

☙

_____

_____

_____

_____

_____

_____

_____

~Prayer: Thank You Lord for allowing me to be a partaker of Your peace through divine relationship with You.

Day 41

And unto man he said, Behold, the fear of the Lord, that is wisdom; and to depart from evil is understanding.

Job 28:28 KJV

Thank You Lord,

You grant wisdom and understanding to all that seek Your face. Thank You for the knowledge that insight and perception are directly tied to our obedience and willingness to shun evil. Thank You for being a rewarder to them that diligently seek You. Amen.

 C3

_____

_____

_____

_____

_____

_____

_____

~**Prayer**: Thank You Lord for granting me wisdom and understanding.

Day 42

Preserve me, O God: for in thee do I put my trust.

Psalm 16:1 KJV

Thank You Lord,

You preserve us and we can depend on You. You are always there for us and never change. You will never leave us nor forsake us. Man cannot give us such solitude. Man is flaky at best. You are constant in our lives and we put our trust solely in You. Amen.

☙

_____

_____

_____

_____

_____

_____

_____

~Prayer: Thank You Lord for preservation I can trust.

Day 43

For thou wilt light my candle: the Lord my God will enlighten my darkness. . .
[29]For by thee I have run through a troop; and by my God have I leaped over a wall.

Psalm 18:28-29 KJV

Thank You Lord,

You enable us to run through troops and leap over walls! When discouragement comes, we can know that it means You're about to do a great work on our behalf. Thank You for causing us to be mighty, for lighting our candles, for bringing us out of darkness, and for ensuring that we have the strength needed for every situation. Amen.

CB

_____

_____

_____

_____

_____

_____

_____

_____

~Prayer: Thank You Lord for equipping me with enduring strength.

Day 44

Who shall ascend into the hill of the Lord? or who shall stand in his holy place?
[4]He that hath clean hands, and a pure heart; who hath not lifted up his soul unto vanity, nor sworn deceitfully.

Psalm 24:3-4 KJV

Thank You Lord,

You have provided instruction on how to ascend toward Your holy place. We stand before You with clean hands and hearts full of praise. Thank You for accepting our lives as sacrifices worthy of dwelling in Your kingdom. Now rest, rule and abide with us forevermore. Amen.

☙

_____

_____

_____

_____

_____

_____

_____

~Prayer: Thank You Lord for teaching me the path to You.

Day 45

Who shall ascend into the hill of the Lord? or who shall stand in his holy place? ⁴He that hath clean hands, and a pure heart; who hath not lifted up his soul unto vanity, nor sworn deceitfully. ⁵He shall receive the blessing from the Lord, and righteousness from the God of his salvation.

Psalm 24:3-5 KJV

Thank You Lord,

You are able to separate us from anything that bars us from giving You true worship! We come before You seeking personal relationship rather than opportunities to be seen by others who lack Your power. We come seeking the fullness of life with You. We offer You our blessings and in return receive Your righteousness and salvation. Amen.

ॐ

_____

_____

_____

_____

_____

_____

_____

~**Prayer**: Thank You Lord for giving me the opportunity to bless You.

Day 46

One thing have I desired of the Lord, that will I seek after; that I may dwell in the house of the Lord all the days of my life, to behold the beauty of the Lord, and to enquire in his temple.

Psalm 27:4 KJV

Thank You Lord,

You are available to us daily. We can steal away and You will be our refuge from the worldly situations that attempt to consume us. Thank You for the hiding place You provide. Nothing compares to You. Amen.

CB

_____

_____

_____

_____

_____

_____

_____

~Prayer: Thank You Lord for allowing me to dwell in Your temple.

Day 47

I will extol thee, O Lord; for thou hast lifted me up, and hast not made my foes to rejoice over me. ²O Lord my God, I cried unto thee, and thou hast healed me.

Genesis 1:31 KJV

Thank You Lord,

You are an encourager that lifts our spirits and reassures us. Thank You for hearing our cries and for working all things together in our favor. Thank You for opening doors that had been closed to us. Your faithfulness unto us is underserved. Yet, You still allow us to rejoice – and we are thankful. Amen.

CB

_____

_____

_____

_____

_____

_____

_____

_____

~Prayer: Thank You Lord for faithfulness to me when I am unworthy.

Day 48

I will bless the Lord at all times: his praise shall continually be in my mouth.
Psalm 34:1 KJV

Thank You Lord,

You make us able to rejoice! You are worthy of praise. We could never repay You for all of the ways in which You have blessed our lives. The most we can do is to continually offer praise. Thank You, Oh Lord, for caring for us. We bless You. Amen.

☙

_____

_____

_____

_____

_____

_____

_____

~**Prayer**: Thank You Lord for receiving my praise.

Day 49

Many are the afflictions of the righteous: but the Lord delivereth him out of them all.

Psalm 34:19 KJV

Thank You Lord,

You are our constant help against rude, hateful and deceitful people. Thank You that You build fences around us. As long as we keep our eyes on You, we can experience freedom from persecution. You never promised us that afflictions would not come, but rather, that they would not devour us. Help us to remain content as You go to battle for us. Amen.

☙

_____

_____

_____

_____

_____

_____

_____

_____

~**Prayer**: Thank You Lord for removing all of my afflictions.

Day 50

Cast thy burden upon the Lord, and he shall sustain thee: he shall never suffer the righteous to be moved.

Psalm 55:22 KJV

Thank You Lord,

We can rely on You. We never have to worry because You cover and keep us in Your care. Continue to help us remember to let go of what the hymn writer described as "the needless pains we bear all because we do not carry everything to You in prayer." Amen.

❦

_____

_____

_____

_____

_____

_____

_____

_____

~**Prayer**: Thank You Lord for being my burden bearer.

Day 51

In God have I put my trust: I will not be afraid what man can do unto me.

Psalm 56:11 KJV

Thank You Lord,

We are able to put our trust in You. We have no reason to fear because You have conquered everything – even death! Fear represents a lack of trust. We fear not because You are our provider, healer, deliver and You give us peace. There is no greater power than You. Amen.

℘

_____

_____

_____

_____

_____

_____

_____

_____

~**Prayer**: Thank You Lord for creating an atmosphere in which I never need to be afraid.

Day 52

Let them be confounded and consumed that are adversaries to my soul; let them be covered with reproach and dishonour that seek my hurt. [14]*But I will hope continually, and will yet praise thee more and more.*

Psalm 71:13-14 KJV

Thank You Lord,

You have allowed us to have continual hope because You care so very deeply for us. You are the God of our salvation and are forever concerned about what concerns us. Amen.

ᙢ

_____

_____

_____

_____

_____

_____

_____

~**Prayer**: Thank You Lord for giving me continual hope.

Day 53

For he satisfieth the longing soul, and filleth the hungry soul with goodness.
                                                        Psalm 107:9 KJV

Thank You Lord,

You satisfy the believer. We meditate on Your word both day and night as this pleases You. Thank You for filling our voids, our empty places. Thank You for quenching our thirst and feeding our hungry souls. We long for You, Lord. Amen.

CB

_____

_____

_____

_____

_____

_____

_____

_____

~**Prayer**: Thank You Lord for the satisfaction that only a life with You can give.

Day 54

Blessed are the undefiled in the way, who walk in the law of the Lord.

Psalm 119:1 KJV

Thank You Lord,

You meet us where we are. You wrap Your loving arms around us and care for us. You honor the willingness in us to obey the word of God. As we give way to You; comfort, rest and divine blessings are poured out on our lives. Amen.

℥

_____

_____

_____

_____

_____

_____

_____

_____

~Prayer: Thank You Lord for blessing me as I seek to know You.

Day 55

I will run the way of thy commandments, when thou shalt enlarge my heart.
Psalm 119:32 KJV

Thank You Lord,

You fully understand our desire to be holy. Continue perfecting us until the day that we meet face to face. We thank You for renewing our hearts and spirits daily. You give us clean hearts to serve Thee. In return, our desire is to please You. Amen.

 C3

_____

_____

_____

_____

_____

_____

_____

~Prayer: Thank You Lord for giving me a heart for You.

Day 56

Yea, the darkness hideth not from thee; but the night shineth as the day: the darkness and the light are both alike to thee.

Psalm 139:12 KJV

Thank You Lord,

You are omnipresent. Even in our darkest hours, You are here. What a blessed relief it is to know that You never leave. Whether we exhibit the light of You or have a dark moment, Your love for us never waivers. When we are happy, sad, fearful, mad . . . whatever we are going through, You remain constant. Amen.

CB

_____

_____

_____

_____

_____

_____

_____

~Prayer: Thank You Lord that Your love for me never waivers.

Day 57

Search me, O God, and know my heart: try me, and know my thoughts. [24]*And see if there be any wicked way in me, and lead me in the way everlasting.*
Psalm 139:23-24 KJV

Thank You Lord,

You know us and nothing can be hidden from You. You know whether we have been obedient or not; have fallen astray or not; are listening for Your voice or not, etc. You know that our flesh is weak and provide a mechanism for keeping us on track. You help us to avoid a disastrous end. You lead us toward the cross! Amen.

CB

_____

_____

_____

_____

_____

_____

_____

_____

~Prayer: Thank You Lord for leading me toward everlasting life.

Day 58

Trust in the Lord with all thine heart; and lean not unto thine own understanding.

Proverbs 3:5 KJV

Thank You Lord,

You've taught us to have the faith of a child that depends solely on his or her parents. You've shown through Your word and actions toward us that we can believe You. Often we can make no carnal sense of what You are showing us, but come to find that it is divinely accurate. Thank You that Your thoughts are not like ours, but instead are Holy. Amen.

❧

_____

_____

_____

_____

_____

_____

_____

~**Prayer**: Thank You Lord that Your thoughts are not like mine.

Day 59

Keep thy heart with all diligence; for out of it are the issues of life.

Proverbs 4:23 KJV

Thank You Lord,

You are able to make us living vessels of Your love. Thanks for the example we have to follow of choosing to uplift others, to speak words of life, hope and healing over our brothers and sisters. Thank You for teaching us the value of embracing a sacred spirit. Thank you for renewing our hearts and allowing us to carry You with us along our individual journey. Amen.

ॐ

_____

_____

_____

_____

_____

_____

_____

_____

~**Prayer**: Thank You Lord for using me as Your vessel.

Day 60

Can a man take fire in his bosom, and his clothes not be burned?

Proverbs 6:27 KJV

Thank You Lord,

You are just to forgive and to help us every time we stumble. Thank You for grace and the loving hand of mercy continually extended toward us – especially because we do not deserve these things. Thank You for being an awesome God. Amen.

CB

_____

_____

_____

_____

_____

_____

_____

~**Prayer**: Thank You Lord for continually forgiving my shortcomings.

Day 61

In the multitude of words there wanteth not sin: but he that refraineth his lips is wise.

Proverbs 10:19 KJV

Thank You Lord,

You've taught us in Your word to use our words wisely – to promote unification rather than to tear others down. You've taught us to remove ourselves from lying, gossiping and other harmful speech. Even further, this message examines the beauty in simply refraining to speak at all. Thank You for teaching us the sheer wisdom in being quiet; in not always saying what comes to mind. Thank You for helping us to see the connection between silence and "sinlessness". Amen.

༃

_____

_____

_____

_____

_____

_____

_____

_____

~**Prayer**: Thank You Lord for admonishing me to show restraint.

Day 62

There is a way which seemeth right unto a man, but the end thereof are the ways of death.

Proverbs 14:12 KJV

Thank You Lord,

You have completely outlined a way of living that keeps us both at peace and in right standing with You. We also know that there can be *temporary* contentment for those who live outside of Your will. Thank You for showing us the path to perfect peace as well as the path to salvation and life. Thank You for helping us to avoid the death of spirit that is sure to come for those who choose to deny You. Amen.

ധ

_____

_____

_____

_____

_____

_____

_____

~Prayer: Thank You Lord helping me to avoid death of spirit.

Day 63

A merry heart maketh a cheerful countenance: but by sorrow of the heart the spirit is broken.

Proverbs 15:13 KJV

Thank You Lord,

Trails have come into our lives disguised as opportunities for You to deliver us. Thank You for the ability to cast every care upon You. Because of You, dark clouds can go away, tears can be dried from our eyes, our heads can be lifted and our feet can once again be firmly planted -- trusting that we are divinely liberated from sorrow. Amen.

℘

_____

_____

_____

_____

_____

_____

_____

_____

~Prayer: Thank You Lord for freeing me from sorrow.

Day 64

Better is little with the fear of the Lord than great treasure and trouble therewith.
Proverbs 15:16 KJV

Thank You Lord,

Discipline teaches us to be content with what You have provided knowing that every need has been taken care of indefinitely. The Bible instructs us to worry not what we shall eat nor drink! In Your mercifulness, many times You have provided beyond what we need and have also granted us the desires of our hearts. In all things we give thanks. Amen.

Cß

_____

_____

_____

_____

_____

_____

_____

~**Prayer**: Thank You Lord that I can experience contentment.

Day 65

A merry heart doeth good like a medicine: but a broken spirit drieth the bones.
Proverbs 17:22 KJV

Thank You Lord,

You prove to be a source of strength during times of upheaval or calamity. We can find joy in disappointment if we simply bow in faithful prayer and wait to see the manifestation of Your will in any situation. You are in control of everything. The more we trust You and avoid allowing the negativity of the situation to overtake us, the merrier are our hearts! Amen.

CB

_____

_____

_____

_____

_____

_____

_____

_____

~**Prayer**: Thank You Lord that I can have a merry heart in difficult times.

Day 66

He that goeth about as a talebearer revealeth secrets: therefore meddle not with him that flattereth with his lips.

Proverbs 20:19 KJV

Thank You Lord,

For divine wisdom and instruction – which You freely give to us all. In scripture You have warned us about the character traits to avoid – both to become better individuals and to also know when we have come into contact with those who intend to do us or others harm. Amen.

CB

_____

_____

_____

_____

_____

_____

_____

_____

~**Prayer**: Thank You Lord for warning me about wrong character traits.

Day 67

I went by the field of the slothful, and by the vineyard of the man void of understanding; ³¹*And, lo, it was all grown over with thorns, and nettles had covered the face thereof, and the stone wall thereof was broken down.*

Proverbs 24:30-31 KJV

Thank You Lord,

You have filled our days with work, chores and tasks to complete. Thank You also for education that is available so that we can continue to learn and grow in wisdom. Thank You for challenges that arise as opportunities to think and respond in ways that keep our minds strong. Thank You that we don't have to be void of understanding or lacking in knowledge. Amen.

☙

_____

_____

_____

_____

_____

_____

_____

_____

~Prayer: Thank You Lord I am growing in wisdom and knowledge.

Day 68

Where no wood is, there the fire goeth out: so where there is no talebearer, the strife ceaseth.

Proverbs 26:20 KJV

Thank You Lord,

For the relationships we have that are grounded in Your light, love and peace! Thank You for instructing us to surround ourselves with family, friends, associates, colleagues and others that lift us up. Equally, we are asked to put a safe distance between those who harbor strife. We are reminded to pray for our brothers and sisters living tumultuous lives full of chaos and turmoil. Amen.

☯

_____

_____

_____

_____

_____

_____

_____

~**Prayer**: Thank You Lord for the ability to forge my own positive relationships.

Day 69

He that covereth his sins shall not prosper: but whoso confesseth and forsaketh them shall have mercy.

Proverbs 28:13 KJV

Thank You Lord,

You have provided a path for us to confess our sins and to be forgiven. Lord, we understand that no one is perfect but You. We will make mistakes. We will fall short at times. Thank You for a continuing path to righteousness and that we can never be completely forbidden from receiving grace. Amen.

ౙ

_____

_____

_____

_____

_____

_____

_____

~Prayer: Thank You Lord for forgiving my transgressions.

Day 70

He, that being often reproved hardeneth his neck, shall suddenly be destroyed, and that without remedy.

Proverbs 29:1 KJV

Thank You Lord,

You chastise us when we go against Your commandments. Thank You for the rod of correction extended to us as a means of protection. We know that You chastise us because You love us and want to see us prosper by living fully in the truth rather than suffer from the consequences of living outside of Your will. Amen.

ের

_____

_____

_____

_____

_____

_____

_____

~**Prayer**: Thank You Lord correcting me when I am wrong.

Day 71

Behold, thou art fair, my love; behold, thou art fair.

Song of Solomon 1:15 KJV

Thank You Lord,

That You speak words of encouragement to us. We don't have to rely on praise and accolades from others that often won't come due to jealousy, spite or envy. Thank You that we can commune with You, accept Your love and encouragement and be ushered into a greater destiny. The encouragement that can only come from You makes us greater, better, fuller and more ready to do Your will. Amen.

☙

_____

_____

_____

_____

_____

_____

_____

~Prayer: Thank You Lord for encouraging me toward a greater trajectory.

Day 72

My beloved spake, and said unto me, Rise up, my love, my fair one, and come away.

Song of Solomon 2:10 KJV

Thank You Lord,

For the ability to steal away from the trials and tribulations of this world. We can abide in You – even hide in Your safety – knowing that You welcome us to do so. Thank You that You desire quiet time with us in sweet communion. Amen.

☙

_____

_____

_____

_____

_____

_____

_____

_____

~**Prayer**: Thank You Lord I can spend private time in Your presence.

Day 73

If ye be willing and obedient, ye shall eat the good of the land.

Isaiah 1:19 KJV

Thank You Lord,

For the opportunity to obey Your word. Thank you for the assurance that if we operate in the Will of God and obey Your word, no good thing will be withheld from us. Thank You also that, even in the areas that challenge us; the areas that continually cause us to sin and to fall short of Your glory, You are diligent to forgive and to strengthen. Thank You that when we seek to move forward with our own plans and agendas, Your loving hand of correction will pull us back, restore and deliver us. Amen.

ଔ

_____

_____

_____

_____

_____

_____

_____

~Prayer: Thank You Lord for rewarding my obedience.

Day 74

Cast thy bread upon the waters: for thou shalt find it after many days.

Ecclesiastes 11:1 KJV

Thank You Lord,

When we feel alone or as if our needs may not get met, we are reminded of the sweet blessedness of life with You. Thank You that You are continually making ways for us, even working miracles on our behalf. You specialize at working all situations together for our good. Amen.

CЗ

_____

_____

_____

_____

_____

_____

_____

~Prayer: Thank You Lord that all of my needs are met and I never experience lack.

Day 75

Also I heard the voice of the Lord, saying, Whom shall I send, and who will go for us? Then said I, Here am I; send me.

Isaiah 6:8 KJV

Thank You Lord,

For the ability to "rightfully divide the word of truth", to tell others about Your goodness and to live a life of faith. Thank You for divine revelation that continues to grant us the wisdom and knowledge to serve as representatives of Your kingdom. Amen.

 CB

_____

_____

_____

_____

_____

_____

_____

~Prayer: Thank You Lord for calling me to a life of service.

Day 76

Thou wilt keep him in perfect peace, whose mind is stayed on thee: because he trusteth in thee.

Isaiah 26:3 KJV

Thank You Lord,

For the incredible peace that comes because we trust You in every situation. Thank You for discernment and the ability to "see" things that others cannot see because we are trusting You to guide us. Thank You that the innate character we embody when we trust You that will ultimately lead others to foster the same type of devotion. Amen.

ᛉ

_____

_____

_____

_____

_____

_____

_____

~**Prayer**: Thank You Lord that I experience peace when I trust You.

Day 77

For thus saith the Lord God, the Holy One of Israel; In returning and rest shall ye be saved; in quietness and in confidence shall be your strength.

Isaiah 30:15 KJV

Thank You Lord,

For the ability to periodically create a sanctuary – a place of retreat – to rest and recharge for the remainder of our journey. Thank You for the sheer strength, clarity and confidence that comes after moments of silence spent in meditation. Amen.

CB

_____

_____

_____

_____

_____

_____

_____

~Prayer: Thank You Lord for causing me to enter into quiet contemplation.

Day 78

And the work of righteousness shall be peace; and the effect of righteousness quietness and assurance forever.

Isaiah 32:17 KJV

Thank You Lord,

For discernment concerning those attempting to hinder our progress, to block our opportunities or to simply frustrate us. Thank You that we can actually bless them that curse us. As we trust You, we can be at total peace no matter what may come our way. Amen.

❧

_____

_____

_____

_____

_____

_____

_____

~**Prayer**: Thank You Lord that I can have peace in times of peril.

Day 79

And my people shall dwell in a peaceable habitation, and in sure dwellings, and in quiet resting places;

Isaiah 32:18 KJV

Thank You Lord,

That we can live in peace simply by completely committing to You instead of going about life on our own terms. We can choose to either forge ahead making mistakes or embrace a life of blessed assurance by allowing You to lead and guide our every decision. Amen.

℘

_____

_____

_____

_____

_____

_____

_____

~Prayer: Thank You Lord that I can securely dwell with You.

Day 80

And wisdom and knowledge shall be the stability of thy times, and strength of salvation: the fear of the Lord is his treasure.

Isaiah 33:6 KJV

Thank You Lord,

We have the ability to study Your word and to gain wisdom as well as understanding. As we hide the word of God in our hearts, we begin to stabilize our lives in meaningful ways as we now have a roadmap for how to handle any given situation. Amen.

൮

_____

_____

_____

_____

_____

_____

_____

~Prayer: Thank You Lord I am being filled with the kind of knowledge and wisdom only salvation can bring.

Day 81

And the parched ground shall become a pool, and the thirsty land springs of
water.

Isaiah 35:7 KJV

Thank You Lord,

Where we are empty, You fill us. Where we thirst, You quench us.
Where we are barren, You cause us to be fertile. Thank You for the
work of the Holy Spirit interceding on our behalf to resurrect areas
of our lives that have been adversely affected. Thank You for the
springs of living water that grant us new life. Amen.

൬

_____

_____

_____

_____

_____

_____

_____

_____

~Prayer: Thank You Lord for completely rearranging my situation.

Day 82

But they that wait upon the Lord shall renew their strength; they shall mount up with wings as eagles; they shall run, and not be weary; and they shall walk, and not faint.

Isaiah 40:31 KJV

Thank You Lord,

We can wait for Your divine provision knowing that it will come at an appointed time! We know that not waiting for You can lead to destruction. We also know that what You have planned for us will be better than any other possible option. Amen.

☙

_____

_____

_____

_____

_____

_____

_____

_____

~**Prayer**: Thank You Lord for giving me a chance to practice trusting You to rescue me at the appropriate time.

Day 83

When the poor and needy seek water, and there is none, and their tongue faileth for thirst, I the Lord will hear them, I the God of Israel will not forsake them.
Isaiah 41:17 KJV

Thank You Lord,

We can drink daily from Your fountain. There we can find sweet communion with the Holy Spirit. The care that You provide in our times of need keeps us on the path of righteousness – knowing that there is no lack and that nothing can harm us. Amen.

℘

_____

_____

_____

_____

_____

_____

_____

~Prayer: Thank You Lord for meeting my needs when others fail.

Day 84

When thou passest through the waters, I will be with thee; and through the rivers, they shall not overflow thee: when thou walkest through the fire, thou shalt not be burned; neither shall the flame kindle upon thee.

Isaiah 43:2 KJV

Thank You Lord,

You make us beacons of Your strength – virtual lighthouses shining brightly for others to see how You are working in our lives. Thank You that even though our lives sometimes have been broken, we are living testimonies of Your faithfulness. Amen.

CB

_____

_____

_____

_____

_____

_____

_____

_____

~**Prayer**: Thank You Lord for making me an example of Your faithfulness.

Day 85

I will go before thee, and make the crooked places straight: I will break in pieces the gates of brass, and cut in sunder the bars of iron.

Isaiah 45:2 KJV

Thank You Lord,

You have gone before us to prepare the way. When there is deceit, danger or destruction in our paths, You have provided clarity. When we have been tested greatly by those things that are attractive to us – opportunities for false love, fake riches or futile friendships – You provide us a way of escape. All we have to do is choose You. Amen.

☙

_____

_____

_____

_____

_____

_____

_____

~**Prayer**: Thank You for always going before me and providing a way of escape!

Day 86

Behold, I have refined thee, but not with silver; I have chosen thee in the furnace of affliction.

Isaiah 48:10 KJV

Thank You Lord,

Our worst day with You is better than our best day on our own. Thank You that ALL things work together for the good of them that love You. We are grateful for the transformative work that is happening in our lives. We yield to Your will and Your way – knowing, even when we are afflicted, deliverance will come. Amen.

☙

_____

_____

_____

_____

_____

_____

_____

~Prayer: Thank You Lord, that even in affliction, I can fully trust You to deliver me!

Day 87

Thus saith the Lord, thy Redeemer, the Holy One of Israel; I am the Lord thy God which teacheth thee to profit, which leadeth thee by the way that thou shouldest go.

Isaiah 48:17 KJV

Thank You Lord,

You are constantly teaching us! We can take comfort that even when we make mistakes, You can still guide us (and even give us a testimony). Thank You that we are simply vessels that carry Your instruction. Amen.

❦

_____

_____

_____

_____

_____

_____

_____

_____

~**Prayer**: Thank You Lord for allowing me to learn from You those things that benefit me most.

Day 88

He is despised and rejected of men; a man of sorrows, and acquainted with grief: and we hid as it were our faces from him; he was despised, and we esteemed him not.

Isaiah 53:3 KJV

Thank You Lord,

When we are despised and rejected by man, we have hope in knowing that no earthly relationship can begin to compare with the love that comes from You. You were supremely rejected – the chief cornerstone that was rejected. We must ask ourselves, "If they did it to You, why should we be any different?" Then we must remember that we are not worthy to even clean Your feet, and yet, You have called us and we are Yours. We are eternally grateful. Amen.

C８

_____

_____

_____

_____

_____

_____

_____

_____

~**Prayer**: Thank You Lord for offering me relationship with You that is so good, it cannot be compared to anything else.

Day 89

For my thoughts are not your thoughts, neither are your ways my ways, saith the Lord.

Isaiah 55:8 KJV

Thank You Lord,

We are able to give everything over to You. You are able to see things differently than we do and are constantly working on our behalf whether we deserve it or not. When our limited minds and ability won't allow us to handle a situation, You come in with fresh perspective, Godly perspective, that meets our situation. Amen.

೮෫

_____

_____

_____

_____

_____

_____

_____

~**Prayer**: Thank You Lord that You know exactly what to do for me.

Day 90

So shall My word be that goes forth from My mouth; It shall not return to Me void, But it shall accomplish what I please, And it shall prosper in the thing for which I sent it.

Isaiah 55:16-18 KJV

Thank You Lord,

You have spoken over each of us and have called us to be great in the way You desire. We can rest in faith knowing that Your word is true. You will accomplish in each of us what You have already made provision for. As we incline our hearts and minds toward You, all of our needs will be met. We must only share Your divinity with others through the words that we speak and the lives that we live. Amen.

൪

_____

_____

_____

_____

_____

_____

_____

_____

~Prayer: Thank You Lord for graciously giving me ALL I need!

CꙄ

INDEX

55	Righteousness	55
3	Sacrifice	3
27	Sacrifice	27
5	Salvation	5
6	Salvation	6
7	Salvation	7
39	Salvation	39
57	Salvation	57
80	Salvation	80
53	Satisfaction	53
37	Security	37
75	Service	75
63	Sorrow	63
35	Sustainment	35
28	Trust	28
51	Trust	51
58	Trust	58
86	Trust	86
25	Victory	25
31	Victory	31
22	Wisdom	22
41	Wisdom	41
67	Wisdom	67
89	Wisdom	89
84	Witness	84

ABOUT THE AUTHOR

L. D. Wells is an award winning author, editor, highly regarded public speaker and educator – best known for her work as writer/editor of the *An Anthology of Sisterhood* project. She received a Bachelor of Arts Degree in English from the University of Georgia and also graduated Summa Cum Laude obtaining a Master of Arts Degree in Education with emphasis in Instructional Technology from Central Michigan University.

L. D. Wells is a proud member of Delta Sigma Theta Sorority, Inc. and proudly chairs the Arts and Letters Committee with the Douglas Carroll Paulding Alumnae Chapter. Additionally, she is a Charter Member of the University of Georgia (UGA) Black Alumni Leadership Council, is a member the National Association of Professional Women and volunteers with the Dwight D. and Sheryl H. Howard Foundation. She is the loving and devoted mother to one son, Devon, and is an Atlanta, GA native.

AN **ANTHOLOGY** OF

Sisterhood

A COMPILATION OF
22 Shades of Red

CO-EDITED BY
L. D. WELLS AND FRANCENE BREAKFIELD

FOREWORD BY
RUBY DEE

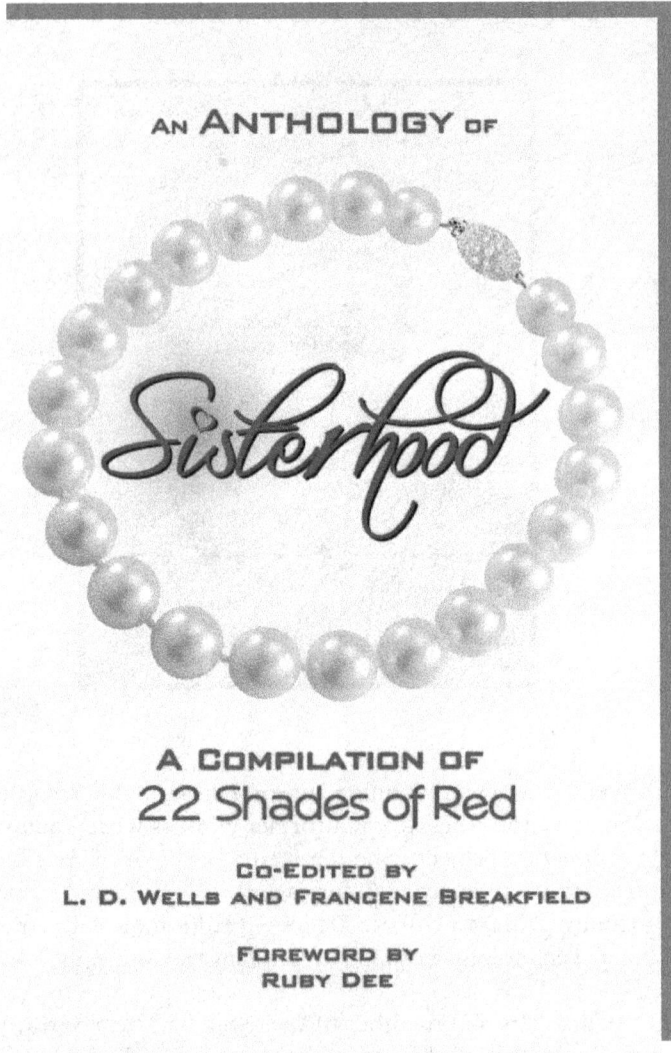

Their masterfully woven stories evoke
the full gamut of the sisterhood experience.
~*The Legendary Ruby Dee*

www.ingramcontent.com/pod-product-compliance
Lightning Source LLC
Chambersburg PA
CBHW071149090426
42736CB00012B/2275